YOUR PASTOR

A Key To Your Personal Wealth

DAVE WILLIAMS

YOUR PASTOR

A Key To Your Personal Wealth

Your Pastor:
A Key To Your Personal Wealth

Copyright ©2001 by David R. Williams

ISBN 0-938020-62-5

This book contains excerpts from "The Pastor's Pay" Copyright ©1989 by David R. Williams and "The Road To Radical Riches" Copyright ©2000 by David R. Williams

First Printing 2001

Published by

DECAPOLIS
PUBLISHING

Printed in the United States of America

MHC   10 9 8 7 6 5 4 3 2

BOOKS BY DAVE WILLIAMS

ABC's of Success and Happiness
AIDS Plague
Beauty of Holiness
Christian Job Hunter's Handbook
Desires of Your Heart
Depression, Cave of Torment
Genuine Prosperity, The Power To Get Wealth
Getting To Know Your Heavenly Father
Gifts That Shape Your Life And Change Your World
Grand Finale Revival
Grief and Mourning
Growing Up in Our Father's Family
Have You Heard From the Lord Lately?
How to Be a High Performance Believer
Laying On of Hands
Lonely in the Midst of a Crowd
The New Life . . . The Start of Something Wonderful
Pacesetting Leadership
The Pastor's Pay
Patient Determination
Revival Power of Music
Remedy for Worry and Tension
Secret of Power With God
Seven Signposts on the Road to Spiritual Maturity
Slain in the Spirit — Real or Fake?
Somebody Out There Needs You
Success Principles From the Lips of Jesus
Supernatural Soulwinning
The Miracle Results of Fasting
The Road To Radical Riches
The World Beyond — The Mysteries of Heaven
Thirty-Six Minutes with the Pastor
Understanding Spiritual Gifts
What To Do If You Miss The Rapture

Contents

"When your heart is generous, your whole life is filled with spiritual understanding."

Introduction

Read This First

You are fed week after week by your pastor. Do you appreciate the commitment he has made to watch over your soul? Most people have no idea of the level of commitment their pastor has made to Christ and to His flock.

Your pastor loves you and spends countless hours praying for you and preparing fresh meals from God's Word for you. Yet some don't show any appreciation at all for all their pastor has done for them and for their families.

In this small book, I'm going to show you how I cheated God's flock for many years without realizing it. I want to make an impact on your life by teaching you how the pastor — the man of God — is an important key to your own personal wealth, and how by honoring him, you can actually be setting your-self up for a financial blessing from God.

Note: I have used the term "man of God" throughout this small book, however, the term is used generically for "man" or "woman" of God.

Never Cheat The Man Of God

Some churches actually cheat their pastor — the man of God.

Uncle Laban cheated his best worker for so long that Jacob finally walked out, leaving him helpless. Jacob was the chief cause of Laban's success and wealth.

Like Jacob, the pastor is largely the cause of the success and income of a church. Sometimes we don't realize what we have ... until we lose it.

> **Let the elders that rule well be counted worthy of double honour, especially they who labour in the word and doctrine. For the scripture saith, Thou shalt not muzzle the ox that treadeth out the corn. And, The labourer is worthy of his re-ward.**
>
> **—1 Timothy 5:17, 18**

What is this Scripture referring to? Read it in the Living Bible, and then trace it out in your cross-ref-erence. You'll see it's clearly referring to taking good care of your pastor.

> Pastors who do their work well should be highly appreciated, especially those who work hard at both preaching and teaching. For the Scriptures say, "Never tie up the mouth of an ox when it is treading out the grain — let him eat as he goes along!" And in another place, "Those who work deserve their pay."
>
> — 1 Timothy 5:17-18 TLB

The pastor has enough pressure points in his ministry. He doesn't need unnecessary financial tensions at home. You want your pastor to be an excellent example to others. To do this, he must have a good home life.

Fifty-six percent of all divorces have their roots in financial tensions.

David E. Roberts, M.D., assistant professor at the University of Tennessee College of Medicine, indicates that incidence of coronary artery disease and high blood pressure is about six times higher for ministers than one would expect in the general population.

I know, the pastor needs to cast his cares on the Lord a little more often. But we're talking about reality here, which sometimes takes a while to catch up to what it should be. Could financial tensions be adding to this problem?

He Should Be Well Dressed

The pastor should be well dressed. He should set an example of distinction. Don't you want to be proud of your pastor? Do you want to bring your friends to church to see a pastor with striped trousers, orange shirt, paisley tie and a checkered sports coat? Is he a pastor or is he a clown?

This is an exaggeration, but clothes do send a message. If the pastor dresses with distinction, people will perceive him to be credible and will hold him in higher regard. People will even give more to the church when their pastor is well dressed. Strange, isn't it? You say, "But God looks on the heart, not the outward appearance."

I answer, "We're not trying to evangelize God."

> But the Lord said unto Samuel, Look not on his countenance, or on the height of his stature; because I have refused him: for the Lord seeth not as man seeth; for man looketh on the outward appearance, but the Lord looketh on the heart.
>
> — 1 Samuel 16:7

Yes, man *does* look on the outward appearance. The Bible simply states that's the way it is. That's why the pastor should look sharp.

He Is On Duty 24 Hours A Day

I believe pastors should do their best to take off one day each week, but sometimes it's not possible.

Sometimes people have special needs, and when they do, their need is their greatest concern, not what day it is.

I remember a night my wife and I planned to spend a quiet, romantic evening together. I had been working a lot of hours, so I was looking forward to the evening. I no sooner stepped into the relaxing, warm bathtub and the phone rang. My wife answered it. I was needed at the hospital, so off I went to be of service. I was glad to do it and my wife understood. But, for the pastor, there is the constant pressure of being on duty 24 hours a day.

It's okay; pastors have answered God's call to this life and expect interruptions. But, shouldn't these dear ones who care so much about us, and bring us the love of Jesus week after week at least be highly esteemed and well-appreciated?

The Pastor's Wife Blesses The Church

Most minister's wives work hard at church—many more hours than a volunteer would.

I do not believe the pastor's wife should work outside of the home and church. She probably works as many hours for the church as her husband does. Even if she works twenty hours and the pastor works sixty, that's eighty hours. It's like two employees for the price of one.

Generally speaking, if a pastor is a sincere man of prayer, is faithful and consistent, and is bearing good fruit, *keep him* — pray for him, pay him well, honor him from time-to-time, and appreciate him as God's gift to the church.

The devil would like to see pastors change churches every three to four years. Experience shows that the fifth, sixth, and seventh years and beyond are normally the most powerful and most productive for the good shepherd who hangs in there with tenacity.

Indicator Of Revival

One of the great indicators of spiritual revival in a person's life is *generosity.* In every massive revival of history, there was a marked increase in the generosity toward ministers and others. When your heart is generous, your whole life is filled with spiritual understanding. A generous attitude causes a giant wave of love to flood your spiritual life. I once heard someone pray:

> "Lord, if I am to err, help me to err on the side of generosity and not the side of stinginess."

I know pastors who now give away 30 to 50 percent of their incomes. This shows their hearts. In fact, I know one well-paid pastor who gives back *more* than what he is paid. He made some good investments over the years, and God has blessed his church with many thousand members and dozens of top Christian business leaders.

Do Unto Others As You Would Like Others To Do Unto You

Therefore all things whatsoever ye would that men should do to you, do ye even so to them for this is the law and the prophets.

— Matthew 7:12

This is the whole matter in a nutshell. Do unto your pastor as you would have done unto you.

Why? Because your pastor is an important key to your personal wealth. I will show you some enlightening scriptural illustrations in the pages ahead.

Why had I missed it for nearly two decades? Why had I cheated God's people out of heavenly blessings that could have been theirs?

I don't know the answer. Perhaps it was pride disguised as humility. I don't know. But thankfully, the Holy Spirit spoke to me through our elders and through my research for the book I wrote entitled *"The Road To Radical Riches."*

Maybe I missed it so you don't have to.

"The man of God is an important key to your personal riches."

Chapter One

Why The Man Of God Is A Key To Your Personal Wealth

One Saturday afternoon I received an urgent phone call from one of our church elders. He said that it was imperative for him to meet with me. Normally nobody disturbs me on Saturdays because they know it's the day I focus on praying for the Sunday services, so whatever the elder wanted, I knew it had to be important. Surprisingly, I had everything done early that day. I was almost finished studying, praying, and getting my sermon written for the next morning when he called. So I suggested we meet at the airport and take a little flight somewhere.

Duane, the elder who called, loves to fly with me, so I thought it would be a nice treat for us to hop in the plane, get above the clouds, and relax a little. He met me at the hanger, but didn't tell me what was so urgent. I guess he was trying to build up his courage first. We gave the plane a pre-flight check, got our clearance, and flew off to a little city southwest of Lansing. We enjoyed our time together.

We landed, parked the plane and went into the airport building for a Coke. After we purchased our colas, we went outside to sit on a bench.

"Okay, Duane," I asked, "What is so important that you would call me on a Saturday?"

"Well, Pastor Dave, we are going to do something tomorrow on Father's Day, and I wanted you to know about it. I never want to do anything behind your back or anything that would embarrass you. The elders and deacons met while you were away on a ministry trip, and we decided that we are going to honor you with a love offering on Father's Day."

"I know how you feel about that," Duane continued. "You haven't allowed us to have a Pastor Appreciation Day in over 16 years, but Pastor Dave, we have heard from God. He has instructed us to take an offering for you tomorrow."

I couldn't believe my ears. I had never allowed any kind of pastor appreciation offering. I've always tried to keep our people focused on Jesus, not me. So my initial response was simply, "No way, Duane."

I Was Cheating My Flock

"But Pastor Dave," Duane reasoned, "you've served for twenty years and the people love you. You've helped many of them to step up from a miserable life to a joyous life in Christ. You are cheating them if you don't allow them to bless you."

When he said, "You are cheating them," it seemed that the Holy Spirit roared in my heart with a force like I hadn't experienced in a long time.

"You *are* cheating them."

I couldn't believe it, but it was true. It hit me like an asteroid. I *had been* cheating my flock out of many blessings by not allowing them to bless me in a visible, substantial way. I felt so foolish and ashamed.

The Holy Spirit began to show me how important it is for people to show their appreciation for the man of God in a tangible way. A slap on the back or a compliment is one thing, but unless there is something tangible attached to it, it can be meaningless and insincere. God showed me that people's wealth depends upon a proper relationship with their spiritual leader. Let me explain.

Opening The Door For Radical Miracles

When Elijah needed food, God commanded a widow woman to sustain him (1 Kings 17a). When she released her meager substance to the prophet, a miracle happened. While famine raged through the land and others were dying, this little widow woman was given a supernatural, inexhaustible supply. She was miraculously able to feed her son, herself, and the prophet throughout the entire famine. By giving to the prophet *first*, she opened a door to personal miracles. Just look.

First, she experienced the miracle of never running out of the necessities of life. Second, when her son became sick and died, the power of God, *working through the prophet*, raised him back to life.

How can you put a price on a child's life? Some say they cannot afford to tithe or to give offerings. But this widow woman experienced the supernatural riches of resurrection power when she needed it. All because she took care of the prophet's needs *first* (1 Kings 17:8-24).

There are people who never do anything for the man who has watched over their souls, prayed for their families, fed them spiritually, and cared for them during the stressful and painful moments of their lives. They have an attitude that says, "We pay him

well enough. We shouldn't be expected to do anything more for the pastor. After all, we don't want to
make him rich, you know. We don't want him to get
proud."

This attitude blocks the miracle power to get
wealth. What if the widow at Zarapheth expressed
that type of attitude? She never would have experienced the miracle of the supernatural supply of food,
and never would have seen God's resurrection power
when her son died.

On the other side of the coin, there are precious
members who actually search for ways to bless their
pastor. They are doing something that is close to
God's heart — something that activates the power to
gain personal wealth.

Every month I get $20 to buy a new tie and a nice
card from somebody who chooses to remain anony-
mous. I don't know who the thoughtful person is,
but I know the door to miracles is opened in his or
her life, just as it was for the widow woman who
blessed the prophet first.

Another lady, who sees me working long hours,
will walk into my office with a hot dinner plate filled
with vegetables, rice and a big T-bone steak. She does
this regularly, and, oh, how it blesses me. It's not the
cost or quality of the meal that blesses me so much.

It's the time I've saved by not having to go out and find some food, especially when I'm heavily involved in a project with a critical deadline. This lady and her family are prospering more and more each year with many miracle blessings. They have work while others are being laid off. They have good things happen to them financially, and they've seen great miracles in their children's lives.

Some people treat the man of God like he's nobody special. Listen, dear friend. The man of God is an important key to *your* personal riches.

After I read 1 Kings 17, the Holy Spirit began to show me how, in the past, I had cheated the people by not allowing them to give to me personally. The precious Spirit of Truth dealt with me as He brought to my attention another illustration of blessing the man of God, and how it brings miracles into the giver's life. We will look at it in the next chapter.

Chapter 2

Blessing The Man Of God

Let's talk about Elijah's successor, Elisha. The prophet traveled through a certain town regularly on his journeys and faced the weary task of finding a place to stay, eat, study, and pray. It probably became quite a strain on him.

A lady in the town was thinking about the prophet one day, and although she didn't know him very well, she invited him over for dinner. What a treat it was for Elisha. Each time he came through town, she would provide him with a terrific meal. Being a thoughtful person, she figured this would ease his burden somewhat. And it did.

Later, she had a discussion with her husband about finding some special way to bless the man of God.

"Honey," she said, "this man is a holy prophet. Let's do something nice for him in a tangible way. We have lots of extra room here. Let's build an apartment onto our home and furnish it for him. That way, whenever he passes through town, he'll have a comfortable place to stay. He can pray here, study, and get some rest, too."

Some people are always thinking of ways to bless the man of God in some practical, tangible, meaningful way.

They built the apartment for Elisha, and, oh how he loved it. He deeply appreciated the kindness of this woman and her husband. One day, he wanted to do something nice for the woman and her husband, so he asked what she would really like. She told him she wanted nothing, that she was perfectly content. So Elisha started doing a little research about the lady.

A Miracle Harvest

While his assistant was digging around for information, he learned that the woman had been unable to have children. She always wanted to have a child, but for some reason or another, was unable to conceive. So Elisha marched downstairs and told the lady, "Next year about this time, you shall have a son!" The following year she had a baby boy, just as Elisha had prophesied. Talk about supernatural wealth. She was blessed because she thought enough of God's man to bless him.

The story doesn't end there. One day her son developed a persistent headache and a fever. You can imagine the anguish of his mother. Then it happened — her worst nightmare. The boy stopped breathing and died.

Now the door to miracles was open to her family because of the way they had taken care of the prophet of God. Elisha laid himself over the boy's lifeless, cold body and commanded the breath of life to re-enter him. After a little while, the boy's cold flesh became warm, he sneezed, and woke up from death.

That's real wealth. Helping the man of God was a small price for her to pay for having the supernatural power of God available when she needed it (2 Kings 4:8-37).

In studying these cases, it almost seems that God provides a special miracle-like benefit to the children of parents who honor the man of God. I never saw the connection until doing this particular study, but I've noticed it over the years and wondered why. Now I know.

Children of those who *do not* honor the pastor, evangelist, or church officials, seem to fall prey to the enemy. Some can't find jobs, others become un-dependable, still others experience tragedy or heart-ache in one form or another, and some just go into flagrant wickedness and are lost.

But the children of those who honor the man of God seem to flow in miracles and have good things happen in their lives continually. They are vibrant, well balanced, respectful, and enjoy a great relation-ship with their parents and with God.

Bless Your Pastor In A Tangible Way

When I read these passages in 1 Kings 17 and 2 Kings 4, I began to understand how important it is for church members to do something tangible for their pastors. These men of God are often taken lightly. Carnal men somehow get on the church deacon's board and often try to jerk the pastor around and frus-trate his vision.

These pastors are shepherds; on duty 24 hours a day. They preach and teach and are more committed than most people will ever realize. They are usually good men. I did not say *perfect* men, but good men.

A precious pastor and soul-winner in Southfield, Michigan, has helped lift countless lives from the sting of poverty. One day the congregation decided to bless their pastor. They made him sit on the plat-form while people brought heaps of money and laid it at his feet. Before it was over, the pastor was almost buried in cash. Someone said, "All I could see was his head sticking out of the pile."

I'm sure that must have embarrassed this precious brother, but it opened the door to miracles for the people who participated.

Those with jealousy and covetousness will make excuses not to bless the man of God. "He gets a good salary as it is." "Well, we don't want to have another PTL situation on our hands." The list of excuses extends endlessly, but those who really desire to have an open door to God-given miracles and supernatural wealth are the ones who cherish and bless the man of God financially.

The Pastor's Pay Has An Impact On General Church Income

A few years back I thought I was being a good steward by not allowing the board to raise my pay. We were in another building program and had some other important expenses, so I told the board there would be no pastoral salary increase. I did this two years in a row.

Something strange happened. For the two years I did not allow a pastoral pay raise, our church income stagnated. We had been growing in income by 15 to

20 percent each year. But those two years delivered only a two to three percent increase in the church income. During a meeting, one of our dear elders suggested, "I think the problem with the church income is that we haven't given our pastor so much as a cost of living raise. There's some spiritual connection, I think." So they gave me a 10 percent pay increase. Immediately, the church income went back to growing by 15 to 20 percent. It's almost as if God blesses the church that blesses their pastor.

Your Wealth Is Connected To Your Attitude Toward Anointed Leaders

Your personal wealth is connected with the man of God somehow. After church one Sunday, two ladies were excitedly rejoicing in the foyer about something. I asked them why they were so excited. They said they had heard about my blessing after I had made that $10,000 faith promise to the Kosovo project. "Pastor, we heard about your $80,000 harvest and we are so blessed. We pray every day for God to prosper you. We know that you are the head of this church and when the financial blessings hit the head, they will soon be dripping down to the rest of us!"

I understood what they were saying. I know Jesus Christ is the Head of His worldwide, universal Church, but the pastor is the head of the local church. When the Old Testament priests were anointed, oil was poured first over their heads. It then trickled down their bodies, right down to their toes. In the same way, if a pastor believes in and experiences radical wealth, it's only a matter of time before it starts trickling down to the flock.

> **The husbandman that laboureth must be first partaker of the fruits.**
>
> — 2 Timothy 2:6

While I was writing a chapter for my book entitled *The Road to Radical Riches*, Cheryl Salem called me. Harry and Cheryl Salem are two of our most precious friends in all the world. Cheryl was Miss America 1980, and Harry served many years as the vice president of Oral Roberts Ministries. Today they minister all around the country with their family.

We talked for about forty minutes when suddenly she began to prophesy. She said that a fresh anointing for wealth and supernatural riches was upon me. She said, as I accept it, this anointing is going to flow down to the rest of the body in my church. She then quoted Psalm 133:2.

> **It is like the precious ointment upon the head, that ran down upon the beard, even Aaron's beard: that went down to the skirts of his garment;**
>
> — Psalm 133:2

To be frank, I never realized what an important key I was to people's wealth. But it reminded me that exactly two years previously, from the time I wrote that book on radical riches, Mary Jo and I sat in a car with Dick and Betty Mills. We had just enjoyed a meal together and were saying good night when Dick, under a sudden inspiration, began to make a prophecy over my wife and me. He said that in 24 months, God was going to open the floodgates to an anointing of wealth in our lives. He proceeded to say how this "wealth anointing" would flow *out from us* into our entire church body and how God would give each *believing* member the keys to receiving it.

And it has happened as Dick prophesied!

Chapter 3

Giving Your Way Out Of Poverty

Neville McDonald, a faith-filled pastor in Constantia, South Africa, now serving as pastor of Melodyland Christian Center in California, proved that by honoring the man of God people could break the spirit of poverty.

Neville established a powerful church, winning thousands of poor people to Christ. The church grew to several thousand members over the years. I have personally preached in many places and churches in South Africa, but never any place like Good Hope Christian Center where Neville was pastoring.

South Africans Grow In Wealth

In my many missionary trips to South Africa, not one church ever received an offering for me, except

Neville's church. I couldn't believe they would receive an offering for me. This was new to me. I came to bless their church and didn't expect an honorarium, or a love offering, from them.

I told Neville, "Please, my dear brother, don't give me an offering. I came to bless you, not to receive a gift from you."

He turned around and pointed his finger at me, and I will never forget his words until the day I leave this earth.

"Listen, Dave. Many of these people are poor. The only way to get them out of poverty is to teach them to give their way out. You are a great man of God, and *you will* take this offering from our people. If you refuse, you will cheat them out of their own blessing of wealth."

That was enough of a lecture for me. I knew what he said was true, but I was trying to be "spiritual" by not wanting to receive their offering. But I wasn't being spiritual. I was being stupid. I was actually setting the stage for keeping many of those precious people in poverty. Needless to say, I took their love offering and thanked them from my heart as I prayed a miracle blessing over their lives.

Because the people who attend Neville's church have been taught to tithe, give offerings, and to honor the man of God, many of them are prospering and experiencing miracles in their lives.

In fact, one of the ladies from the church was robbed one day by a dreaded gangster, one who was known to never leave a living witness. She knew her rights. In fact, she told God as she was being held at gun point, "Lord, I am a tither, I give offerings, and I have always shown honor to your servants. Therefore, the devourer is rebuked and no harm shall come to me." She started quoting Scriptures and the robber ended up running off waving his gun but never harming her.

> **The Lord shall cause thine enemies that rise up against thee to be smitten before thy face: they shall come out against thee one way, and flee before thee seven ways.**
>
> **— Deuteronomy 28:7**

Cheating The Man Of God

Those who are constantly trying to figure out ways to cheat the man of God, keep him poor and humble, or hurt him are the same people who will not have the faith they need in time of their trouble.

> **Touch not mine anointed, and do my prophets no harm.**
>
> **— 1 Chronicles 16:22**

It seems that there are those who always seek to hurt the man of God with their endless gossip, contention, complaining, and jealousy. Others seek to bless their pastor with kind words, support, prayers, and tangible giving. Like everything else in life, it's a choice.

Always Bless The Man Of God

Pastors should not have to carry the unnecessary burden of personal financial pressures. They shouldn't have to supplement their income by selling Bibles or getting involved in multi-level marketing programs (1 Timothy 5:17, 18). Pastors need to focus on studying God's Word and praying for the people (Acts 6:4).

The Bible teaches us that we honor God by giving (Proverbs 3:9-10). We honor a pastor the same way — by giving, not only to the church, but also *to him personally.* This opens the door to personal miracles. Even Jesus had certain people who supported him with their substance (Luke 8:1-3).

Appreciating Your Pastor

A dear friend of mine went to the poverty-stricken people of Detroit to reach them for Christ. He could be a pastor anywhere, but he chose to go to the poor. One by one, he led thousands to Jesus. In the process, he was stabbed several times and almost gave his life trying to reach those people who are so precious to God's heart.

Well, he reached them all right. Not only did he lead them to salvation in Christ, he started teaching them the biblical principles of prosperity and abundance. When you listen to a man of faith, it's going to have an effect. Those people started prospering, just as the Bible declares. Oh yes, there are always critics and opponents to any biblical revelation, but those dear people in my friend's church listened to their pastor instead of the critics.

They tithed. They gave offerings. They honored their pastor with a good salary, but they didn't stop there. One night, after a particularly stressful time in their pastor's life, they decided to have a "Pastor Appreciation Day."

They were grateful that their pastor had the courage to teach them the full counsel of God's Word and didn't fool around when it came to teaching them about tithing and prosperity. Many of them had been lifted up from poverty to prosperity because their pastor relentlessly taught them the keys to radical wealth. So they wanted to honor him.

The church gathered a love offering for their pastor. Now think of it. All these so-called "poor" people; the "down-and-outers," took an offering for the man who led them to Christ, prayed for them, and boldly taught them how to break the spirit of poverty.

That love offering for their pastor was counted and ended up being a six-digit figure! That's right. Over $100,000 from people who once were known as Detroit's "poor." Imagine that. What a blessing for my pastor friend to be able to take a nice vacation with his wife, buy a new car, and give more money to his favorite missions project.

I don't need to tell you that the people of that church are happy, prosperous people who are on their way to personal wealth. Many of them knew nothing but poverty all their lives ... until the man of God told them the truth about money, tithing, giving and receiving.

The Man Of God Is One Of Your Keys To Personal Riches

Jesus said it. You cannot serve two masters. You cannot serve both God and mammon. Those who are racing toward true personal wealth refuse to give heed to the foul spirit of mammon. They listen only to the voice of God. Well, here from the Bible, is the voice of God on how to bless the man of God. Never forget the fact that he is an important key to your prosperity.

> Those who are taught in the Word of God should help their teachers by paying them. Don't be misled; remember that you can't ignore God and

get away with it; a man will always reap just the
kind of crop he sows!

— Galatians 6:6-7 TLB

Pastors who do their work well should be paid
well and should be highly appreciated, especially those who work hard at both preaching
and teaching. The Scriptures say, "Never tie up
the mouth of an ox when its treading out the
grain – let him eat as he goes along!" And in
another place, "Those who work deserve their
pay."

— 1 Timothy 5:17,18,25 TLB

Believe in the Lord your God, so shall ye be established; believe His prophets, so shall ye prosper.

— 2 Chronicles 20:20b

It's true. The man of God is a key to your own
personal wealth.

"Only those who are filled with jealousy and covetousness will offer excuses for not blessing the man of God."

Chapter 4

Honor The Man Of God Properly

Now if you want to honor your pastor, please do it right. Don't let it be a slip-shod, spur of the moment, sloppy surprise. I suppose that's better than nothing, but it would be really great if you would take the time to plan out a special day to show your appreciation. You could even enlarge some fun pictures of the pastor and his family and post them around the church building to announce a Pastor Appreciation Day.

First of all, during the service, before you take an offering, share with the congregation some of your pastor's achievements and accomplishments. Arrange to have a few short testimonies of how his or her ministry has impacted lives. Show a three-minute video of the more tender moments in your pastor's life, if possible. Make sure all the church leadership, deacons, and elders take part in this special tribute.

Someone in leadership should talk about the things you've read about in this book. Share with the congregation the principles used in the lives of those two women who blessed Elijah and Elisha, and what the miraculous results were. Assure the people that by honoring God's man, you are honoring God Himself.

Make sure the offering is *specifically for the pastor.* If he wants to give it to missions, that's his business. If he wants to buy a new car, leave that up to him. Receive a good, joyful offering and really bless the man of God. He is an important key to the health and wealth of the church and its membership. Do it, but do it right.

Dr. LeRoy Thompson, in his excellent book, *Money, Thou Art Loosed,* talks about this important key of honoring the man of God. Here's what he says:

> In every church where I preach, I tell the people to see to it that their pastor and his wife are blessed. When you take care of God's things, He will take care of yours. But not esteeming the office of the pastor is one thing that has been holding some people back concerning money.
>
> You see, you have to put first things first.

When you put God first, He will honor and bless you. In other words, when your church is blessed and your pastor has plenty of money in his pocket (without your being critical or concerned about it), then you are in a position for God to give you your increase.

Folks need to release the mentality that the preacher is supposed to be broke. They learned that through certain denominations, and they have the attitude, "the preacher doesn't need very much."

But the truth is, the higher your pastor goes in finances, the higher you can go, too. But if you try to hold him back, the Lord is going to see to it that you are held back, too! (Actually, you will be holding *yourself* back because you're not cooperating with God and His Word.)

So, if you have ever had a bad attitude toward your pastor – if you have ever held your pastor back financially through your attitude and your lack of giving – you can make a little adjustment in your heart today. You can learn to say, and mean from your heart,

"Father, I don't care how high my pastor rises; in fact, I *want* him to prosper and be blessed. I don't care what kind of suit or shoes he wears. I don't care what kind of car he drives. Bless him, Lord. As a matter of fact, Lord, from this day forward, I'm going to get in on Your blessings by helping to make sure my pastor is taken care of."

I would encourage you to order Pastor Thompson's book, *Money, Thou Art Loosed.* You may write to him at: Ever Increasing Word Ministries, P.O. Box 7, Darrow, Louisiana 70725.

Also, my book, *The Pastor's Pay,* is available to you. In it you will discover some important scriptural as well as practical principles for compensating your pastor fairly. You'll find it at your favorite Christian bookstore, or you may order it by calling 1-800-888-7284, or by writing to: The Hope Store, 202 South Creyts Road, Lansing, MI 48917.

The promise of Philippians 4:19, *"But my God shall supply all your need, according to His riches in glory by Christ Jesus,"* was not merely a general promise to everyone who reads it. This promise of a *rich supply* was *specifically* given to those people who had blessed Paul, the man of God, by giving him *more than enough money* to achieve the call of God on his life, and for his personal needs. If you don't believe it, read the entire passage in context (Philippians 4:15-19).

Look For Ways To Bless The Man Of God

Look for ways to bless the anointed man of God. He is a key to your personal wealth.

Zenas and Apollos were planning a missionary trip, being authorized and sent by the Church leadership. Paul endorsed them and encouraged believers to help them financially. He instructed, "Do everything you can to help Zenas the lawyer and Apollos with their trip. *See that they are given everything they need,*" (Titus 3:13 NLT).

There are two key points to emphasize from this Scripture.

(1) Do everything you can to help the man of God.

(2) See to it that he has *everything he needs.* When you do this, Paul infers in the next verse that, as a result, *you* will become more productive.

The man of God is a key to your own wealth. Honor him, esteem him, value him, appreciate him, and love him. Look for ways to bless him, and the blessing will run down to you as well.

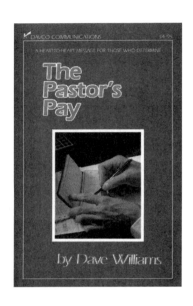

How To Bless Your Pastor

Get a copy for each deacon, elder, trustee, and board member, and for each member of your financial committee. Help bless the man of God!

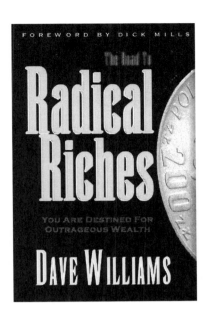

Get On The Road To *RADICAL RICHES!*

No matter who you are, or the messes you made with your money, Dave Williams gives you a step-by-step plan to put you on the road to radical riches. The principles Dave shares in this book work together to provide you with a road map to radical wealth. You are destined for radical wealth! Don't miss your destiny.

- *Your Wealth Containers*
- *The Land Of Abundance And Wealth*
- *How I Know God Wants You Wealthy*
- *The Inexhaustible Supply*
- *Coming Into The Wealthy Place*

$19.95 Each (10 copies 17.95 each, 30 copies $15.95 each)
Available at your favorite bookseller, or by calling (800) 888-7284
or you can write: The Hope Store
202 S. Creyts Rd. Lansing, MI 48917

Prices good while supplies last.

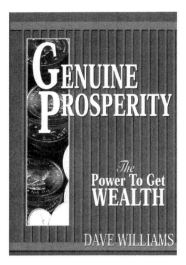

For Your Spiritual Growth

Here's the help you need for your spiritual journey. These books will encourage you, and give you guidance as you seek to draw close to Jesus and learn of Him. Prepare yourself for fantastic growth!

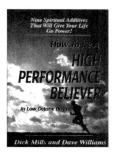

HOW TO BE A HIGH PERFORMANCE BELIEVER
Pour in the nine spiritual additives for real power in your Christian life.

SECRET OF POWER WITH GOD
Tap into the real power with God; the power of prayer. It will change your life!

THE NEW LIFE ...
You can get off to a great start on your exciting life with Jesus! Prepare for something wonderful.

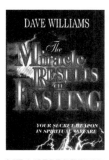

MIRACLE RESULTS OF FASTING
You can receive MIRACLE benefits, spiritually and physically, with this practical Christian discipline.

WHAT TO DO IF YOU MISS THE RAPTURE
If you miss the Rapture, there may still be hope, but you need to follow these clear survival tactics.

THE AIDS PLAGUE
Is there hope? Yes, but only Jesus can bring a total and lasting cure to AIDS.

These and other books available from Dave Williams and:

DECAPOLIS PUBLISHING

For Your Spiritual Growth

Here's the help you need for your spiritual journey. These books will encourage you, and give you guidance as you seek to draw close to Jesus and learn of Him. Prepare yourself for fantastic growth!

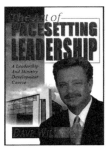
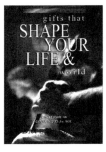
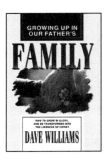

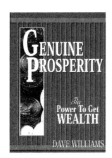

For Your Spiritual Growth

Here's the help you need for your spiritual journey. These books will encourage you, and give you guidance as you seek to draw close to Jesus and learn of Him. Prepare yourself for fantastic growth!

SOMEBODY OUT THERE NEEDS YOU
Along with the gift of salvation comes the great privilege of spreading the Gospel of Jesus Christ.

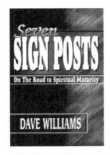

SEVEN SIGNPOSTS TO SPIRITUAL MATURITY
Examine your life to see where you are on the road to spiritual maturity.

THE PASTORS PAY
How much is your pastor worth? Who should set his pay? Discover the scriptural guidelines for paying your pastor.

DECEPTION, DELUSION & DESTRUCTION
Recognize spiritual deception and unmask spiritual blindness.

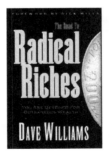

THE ROAD TO RADICAL RICHES
Are you ready to jump from "barely getting by" to God's plan for putting you on the road to Radical Riches?

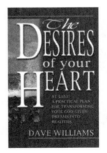

THE DESIRES OF YOUR HEART
Yes, Jesus wants to give you the desires of your heart, and make them realities.

These and other books available from Dave Williams and:

DECAPOLIS PUBLISHING

For Your Successful Life

These video cassettes will give you successful principles to apply to your whole life. Each a different topic, and each a fantastic teaching of how living by God's Word can give you total success!

HOW TO BE A HIGH PERFORMANCE BELIEVER
Pour in the nine spiritual additives for real power in your Christian life.

THE UGLY WORMS OF JUDGMENT
Recognizing the decay of judgment in your life is your first step back into God's fullness.

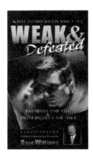

WHAT TO DO WHEN YOU FEEL WEAK AND DEFEATED
Learn about God's plan to bring you out of defeat and into His principles of victory!

WHY SOME ARE NOT HEALED
Discover the obstacles that hold people back from receiving their miracle and how God can help them receive the very best!

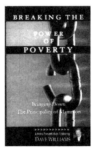

BREAKING THE POWER OF POVERTY
The principality of mammon will try to keep you in poverty. Put God FIRST and watch Him bring you into a wealthy place.

HERBS FOR HEALTH
A look at the concerns and fears of modern medicine. Learn the correct ways to open the doors to your healing.

These and other videos available from Dave Williams and:

DECAPOLIS PUBLISHING

Running Your Race

These simple but powerful audio cassette singles will help give you the edge you need. Run your race to win!

LONELY IN THE MIDST OF A CROWD
Loneliness is a devastating disease. Learn how to trust and count on others to help.

HERBS FOR HEALTH
A look at the concerns and fears of modern medicine. Learn the correct ways to open the doors to your healing.

HOW TO GET ANYTHING YOU WANT
You can learn the way to get anything you want from God!

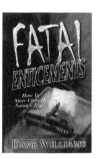

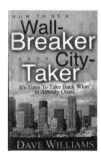

WISHBONE, JAWBONE, BACKBONE
Learn about King David, and how his three "bones" for success can help you in your life quest.

FATAL ENTICEMENTS
Learn how you can avoid the vice-like grip of sin and its fatal enticements that hold people captive.

HOW TO BE A WALL BREAKER AND A CITY TAKER
You can be a powerful force for advancing the Kingdom of Jesus Christ!

These and other audio tapes available from Dave Williams and:

DECAPOLIS PUBLISHING

Expanding Your Faith

These exciting audio teaching series will help you to grow and mature in your walk with Christ. Get ready for amazing new adventures in faith!

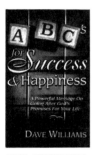

ABC's OF SUCCESS AND HAPPINESS
A powerful message on going after the promises of God.

FORGIVENESS
The miracle remedy for many of life's problems is found in this basic key for living.

UNTANGLING YOUR TROUBLES
You can be a "trouble untangler" with the help of Jesus!

HOW TO BE A HIGH PERFORMANCE BELIEVER
Put in the nine spiritual additives to help run your race and get the prize!

BEING A DISCIPLE AND MAKING DISCIPLES
You can learn to be a "disciple maker" to almost anyone.

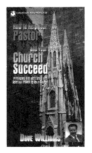

HOW TO HELP YOUR PASTOR & CHURCH SUCCEED
You can be an integral part of your church's & pastor's success.

These and other audio tapes available from Dave Williams and:

DECAPOLIS PUBLISHING

More Products by Dave Williams

BOOK Title

Title	Price
The New Life — The Start Of Something Wonderful	$1.95
End Times Bible Prophecy	$4.95
Seven Sign Posts On The Road To Spiritual Maturity	$4.95
Somebody Out There Needs You	$4.95
Growing Up In Our Father's Family	$4.95
Grief & Mourning	$7.95
The World Beyond — Mysteries Of Heaven	$7.95
The Secret Of Power With God	$7.95
What To Do If You Miss The Rapture	$9.85
Genuine Prosperity	$9.95
The Miracle Results Of Fasting	$9.95
How To Be A High Performance Believer	$9.95
Gifts That Shape Your Life & Change Your World	$10.95
Road To Radical Riches	$19.95

CD Title

Title	Num. of CDs	Price
Middle East Crisis	1	$12.00
Setting Our Houses In Order	1	$12.00
Too Much Baggage?	1	$12.00
Jesus Loves Sinners	1	$12.00
How To Get Your Breakthrough	1	$12.00
Amazing Power Of Desire	1	$12.00
Wounded Spirit	1	$12.00
The Attack On America (Sept. 11, 2001)	1	$12.00
Radical Wealth	5	$60.00

VIDEO Title

Title	Num. of Videos	Price
Going Through Hell	1	$19.95
Acres Of Diamonds — The Valley Of Baca	1	$19.95
120 Elite Warriors	1	$19.95
What To Do If You Miss The Rapture	1	$19.95
Regaining Your Spiritual Momentum	1	$19.95
Herbs For Health	1	$19.95
Destructive Power Of Legalism	1	$19.95
Ugly Worms Of Judgment	1	$19.95
Grief & Mourning	1	$19.95
Breaking The Power Of Poverty	1	$19.95
Triple Benefits Of Fasting	1	$19.95
Why Some Are Not Healed	2	$39.95
Miracle Results Of Fasting	3	$59.95
ABC's For Success And Happiness	3	$59.95
Gifts That Shape Your Life & Change Your World	5	$99.95

AUDIO Title	Num. of Tapes	Price
Lonely In The Midst Of A Crowd	1	$6.00
How To Get Anything You Want	1	$6.00
Untangling Your Troubles	2	$12.00
Healing Principles In The Ministry Of Jesus	2	$12.00
Acres Of Diamonds — The Valley Of Baca	2	$12.00
Finding Peace	2	$12.00
Why People Criticize & Judge	2	$12.00
Judgment On America	2	$12.00
Triple Benefits Of Fasting	2	$12.00
The Day Of Global Confusion	2	$12.00
The Cure For A Broken Heart	2	$12.00
Help! I'm Getting Older	2	$12.00
Regaining Your Spiritual Momentum	2	$12.00
The Destructive Power Of Legalism	2	$12.00
Three Most Important Things In Life	3	$18.00
The Final Series	3	$18.00
The Mysteries Of Heaven	3	$18.00
Dave William's Crash Course In Intercessory Prayer	3	$18.00
Forgiveness — The Miracle Remedy	4	$24.00
How Long Until The End	4	$24.00
What To Do When You Feel Weak And Defeated	4	$24.00
Sin's Grip	4	$24.00
Why Some Are Not Healed	4	$24.00
Bible Cures	4	$24.00
Belial	4	$24.00
God Is Closer Than You Think	5	$30.00
Decoding The Apocalypse	5	$30.00
Winning Your Inner Conflict	5	$30.00
Radical Wealth	5	$30.00
Violent Action For Your Wealth	5	$30.00
The Presence Of God	6	$36.00
Your Spectacular Mind	6	$36.00
The Miracle Results Of Fasting	6	$36.00
Developing The Spirit Of A Conqueror	6	$36.00
Why Do Some Suffer?	6	$36.00
Overcoming Life's Adversities	6	$36.00
Faith Steps	6	$36.00
ABC's For Success & Happiness	6	$36.00
The Best Of Dave Williams	6	$36.00
How To Help Your Pastor & Church Succeed	8	$48.00
Being a Disciple & Making Disciples	8	$48.00
High Performance Believer	8	$48.00
True Or False	8	$48.00
The End Times	8	$48.00
The Beatitudes — Success 101	8	$48.00
Hearing The Voice Of God	10	$60.00
Gifts That Shape Your Life — Personality Gifts	10	$60.00
Gifts That Shape Your Life & Change Your World — Ministry Gifts	10	$60.00
Daniel Parts 1 & 2 (Both Parts 6 Tapes Each)	12	$72.00
Roadblocks To Your Radical Wealth	12	$72.00
Revelation Parts 1 & 2	14	$84.00